THEOD
Hunga
in var
before
the U.   ...though
she grew up on the classics of
English literature, her writing
has been influenced by an Eastern
European literary tradition in
which the boundaries between
realism and the fantastic are often
ambiguous. Her publications
include the short story collection
In the Forest of Forgetting (2006);
Interfictions (2007), a short story
anthology coedited with Delia
Sherman; *Voices from Fairyland*
(2008), a poetry anthology with

critical essays and a selection of her own poems; and *The Thorn and the Blossom* (2012), a novella in a two-sided accordion format. Her work has been translated into nine languages, including French, Japanese, and Turkish. She has been a finalist for the Nebula, Crawford, Locus, Seiun, and Mythopoeic Awards, and on the Tiptree Award Honor List. Her prose-poem "Octavia is Lost in the Hall of Masks" (2003) won the Rhysling Award and her short story "Singing of Mount Abora" (2007) won the World Fantasy Award.

PRAISE FOR *Songs for Ophelia*

"These poems by Theodora Goss are wonderfully nineteenth century and yet modern faerie at the same time. They remind me of the best of the ballads, both the ones from the long tongue-polishing of singers and the ones written by a single poet like Keats' 'Belle Dame Sans Merci'. Not to be missed. Especially the 'Ophelia Cantos'." —Jane Yolen, author of *Sister Fox's Field Guide to Writing, Things to Say to A Dead Man*, and *Owl Moon*

"Willows, dancing maidens, gypsies, mothers, lovers, daughters, magic animals, living waters, and transformations of all kinds abound in these gorgeous poems. With her formal prosody, her fairytale subjects, and her insights on love and loss and longing, Goss manages, Janus-like, to look back to the Victorians and inward at the heart of a modern woman with intelligence and grace." —Delia Sherman, author of *The Freedom Maze* and *Changeling*

Songs for Ophelia

THEODORA GOSS

ISBN 978 1 907881 19 0

Published by Papaveria Press
France

"Beauty to the Beast," *The Lyric*, Summer 1993.
"Molly," *The Lyric*, Fall 2000.
"Chrysanthemums," *Lady Churchill's Rosebud Wristlet* 8, June 2001.
"Helen in Sparta," *Lady Churchill's Rosebud Wristlet* 8, June 2001.
"By Tidal Pools," *Lady Churchill's Rosebud Wristlet* 8, June 2001.
"Falling Boy," *Lady Churchill's Rosebud Wristlet* 9, November 2001.
"The Ophelia Cantos," *Lady Churchill's Rosebud Wristlet* 9, November 2001.
"Autumn, the Fool," *The Lyric*, Fall 2002.
"The Phantom Lover," *The Lyric*, Fall 2002.
"The Bear's Daughter," *Journal of Mythic Arts*, Winter 2003.
"What Her Mother Said," *Journal of Mythic Arts*, Fall 2004.
"The Changeling," *Journal of Mythic Arts*, Winter 2005.
"Nymphs Finding the Head of Orpheus," *Jabberwocky* 1, 2005.
"Goblin Song," MYTHIC, 2006.
"Dirge for a Lady," *October Roses* (CD), 2006.
"The Singer," *October Roses* (CD), 2006.
"The Frost," *October Roses* (CD), 2006.
"Echo and Narcissus," *October Roses* (CD), 2006.
"Bal Macabre," *Mythic Delirium* 15, Summer/Fall 2006.
"The Witch," *Heliotrope*, Fall 2007.
"Fairy Tale," *Journal of Mythic Arts*, Fall 2008.
"The Gentleman," *Mythic Delirium* 21, Summer/Fall 2009.
"As I Was Walking," *Mythic Delirium* 23, Summer/Fall 2010.
"Death," *Mythic Delirium* 23, Summer/Fall 2010.
"Ravens," *Goblin Fruit*, Autumn 2010.
"Binnorie,"*Mythic Delirium* 24, Winter/Spring 2011.
"Vivian to Merlin," *Mythic Delirium* 27, Summer/Fall 2012.
"Shoes of Bark," *Mythic Delirium* 27, Summer/Fall 2012.

WWW.PAPAVERIA.COM

Songs for Ophelia

for Ophelia, of course

Contents

II. Summer Songs

III. Autumn Songs

IV. WINTER SONGS

A Weaponized Elegance

IT IS COMMON TO CALL THE POETRY OF WOMEN OTHERWORLDLY, delicate, elegant. Women, after all, are the delicate sex, the elegantly-souled, otherworldly because we occupy, quite literally in the minds of half the world, another universe full of unguessable motives, muted desires, undecipherable codes. Women who write, most particularly those who write poetry and prose that dances with poetry at the town hall every Friday night, are often critically caged in that pretty prison of otherworldly, delicate, elegant.

And yet, even knowing this, knowing all the power of such words to suffocate in a blanket of analytical lace, when I read Theodora Goss's poems, I keep returning to them. For the collection you hold in your hands is otherworldly, it is elegant, it is delicate. It is graceful, it is exquisite and ethereal. It is full of flowers and fairies and a piercing, thorny longing.

So I will use these words, but I will use them like wishes in a fairy tale: very, very carefully.

These poems *are* otherworldly. They seem to come up out of the pages from another time, from an asteroid floating in the dark, its surface clotted and bound with forests, with luminous flowers, with figures walking under branches that might at any moment becoming grasping hands. They are Romantic poems, drawing the ghosts of Christina Rossetti and William Blake out of Hades by means of spilling their human blood into the great silver bowl of a book. They possess that peculiar, delicious melancholy of paintings on urns, on cameos, of faces and drifting willows constantly bent in thought. They are not savage; they do not seek to be savage, to murder the heart with a scalding line. Rather, they tap the heart with a hundred tiny blows of a glass-maker's hammer until it shatters.

These *are* delicate poems, turned on a jeweler's lathe, their revelations draped as gracefully as Greek cloth. Goss's language fits together like gems in a complex crown, a diadem of images and motifs, resting gently on the head, but with a deceptive weight. Ethereal willows (will I ever know a willow tree in the real world as well as I know the one that changes its leaves through the course of this book?) ponds, moors, woods couple with moments of intensely human, domestic realism (will I ever want a recipe as much as I want to know how to make Wolf Soup, served by a grandmother to a girl in red?) to create achingly genuine scenes.

And they *are* elegant. The elegance of Goss's work has never ceased to amaze me. It feels effortless, but endlessly evocative and suggestive, flowing with the rhythms of both the natural world and the intimate socio-familial cosmos. These poems move through the year as we do, with the grace of inevitability, a familiar series of colors, scents, textures that never ceases to be surprising.

I remember one summer in Budapest, sitting with Theodora Goss and her daughter Ophelia below the tall windows of an apartment across from the National Museum, smelling a storm coming on while the wind whipped through the living room and into the kitchen. Ophelia was reading *The Wizard of Oz*. We could hear violins playing faintly in the square. And I thought then that that moment was like being inside one of Theodora's poems. The wind, the dark clouds, the ozone of the soon-to-be storm, the leaves blowing free, just beginning to singe brown at the edges. Two writers, one per window, with long hair, one black and one red, and long names, one Hungarian and one Italian, lost in their own thoughts, in the books they were planning to write, drinking tea out of Communist-era china, picking at *pogácsa* from the bakery across the street. And all the while a beautiful little girl with pale red hair and great clear eyes reads about Dorothy and that other, more famous storm that blew a child from a world of dust to a world of color. That is what I mean by elegance, the synchronicity of images, the layering of experience and literature, the symmetry of soul and environment. Goss's poems are so full of that elegance that it bleeds into her life, until, in some marvelous moments, there is no difference between a Goss poem and an afternoon spent with her, thinking in unison and companionable quiet. Hers is a weaponized elegance, targeted and unstoppable.

But of course, that can't be right. I must be mistaken. Nothing elegant can be raw. Nothing delicate can break your heart. Nothing otherworldly can say anything real about the human experience. Everyone knows that. It is a universal truth, held universally.

I guess nobody told Theodora Goss. What good fortune for the rest of us.

Catherynne M. Valente

I. Spring Songs

Spring Song

Slowly the willow has turned to silver,
slowly, slowly, over the town,
a shadow has crept – the hint of the season,
the green-gauze hem of Spring's wild gown.

Slowly the river begins to murmur,
slowly I measure the lengthening days,
and the birds return and from high in the budding
trees begin their virelays.

Grasses that cover the graveyard alleys
regain their verdure and windily nod,
and Spring herself sits upon the tombstones,
smiling a smile that is sweet and mad.

Her gown spreads away when the wind is blowing,
a green-gauze net that rides on the air,
and slowly the willow has turned to silver,
and neither she nor I can care.

Theodora Goss

The Willow's Story

The willow was once a bride, and dressed herself in white,
and veiled herself with laces, and blossoms filled her hair,
but her love he rode for London in the middle of the night,
galloping by the churchyard, and left her waiting there.

She wandered by the river, her eyes grown dull and wild,
her satin gown gone ragged, her white feet bruised and bare,
and never spoke nor halted, but went as though beguiled
by fairer visions than appeared in common air.

She threw a bunch of posies her fingers did not hold,
she turned to lift a veil the wind would never stir,
and bowed and smiled, then danced about the rain-drenched wold
in invisible arms, and kissed someone not there.

At last, the story is told, they changed her into a tree,
they being whatever gods possess both pity and power,
so on she silently dances, according to decree,
with the wind for her bridegroom, and the perching birds her dower.

A Storm

The willow is dancing, is dancing in earnest,
above the ripped surface the round lake displays,
unlike the wide privets that stand in fast harness,
responding to motions the wild wind conveys,
while the stones remain steady in silent displays.

Oh, watch her green mane: it is rousing and soaring.
The lake-surface rises and flings out its hands
and grasps at her tendrils, while swift winds are roaring
and scattering rain in successive sharp strands,
and the stones stand immune from their urgent demands.

The Elf King's Daughter

It is the Elf King's daughter,
with the leaf-light in her eyes,
that greenish twilight beneath the beech boughs
where only the hum of flies

disturbs the lilies of the valley
and ferns their fronds unfurl.
How dare I stir or show my presence
to the Elf King's girl?

She sits so still upon the boulder,
the leaf-light in her hair
casting a greenish pall on its goldness.
Mortal, stare

at her small feet shod in leaf-green velvet,
her small hands pale and fay,
among the wood anemones
in early May.

The Bride

Her gown, it seemed a thing made out of mist,
as though the dewy air
had gathered in a cloud about her form
to clothe a shape so fair
that nothing coarser could adorn it than
a layer of atmosphere.

The diamonds in her hair were like the beads
upon a spider's web
that dazzle mayflies in the morning light,
and dangling from each lobe
of her white ears she wore a water-drop
that would weigh down Queen Mab.

She drifted, feather-like, across the lawn
in tenuous radiance
as her three brothers, sporting new frock-coats,
pocketed their pence,
and the ogre stood by the verge of the tenebrous wood
with infinite patience.

What the Ogre Said

Call to the willow,
the willow replies:
the little frogs' eyes
watch you, my darling,
beneath the gray skies,
watch from the hollow,
liquid and yellow,
like jonquils, all guarding
my own pretty prize.

Call to the clouds
and the clouds call again,
to you, pretty girl,
through wind, through rain:
these elegant gauds,
the moon for crown,
and a starry gown,
are yours, my pearl,
my lily, my own.

Call to the river,
the river responds,
gurgling, the giver
of rivulets, ponds,
floods and slim trickles,
irregular bubbles
blown by small fishes:
I'll tend to your wishes,
as burbling it bounds.

Call to me, darling,
I'll make you an answer
you cannot despise,
the wildest romancer
with loveliest lies
inspired by your eyes,
surprisingly charming,
my pretty, my starling,
my sorrowful prize.

The River's Daughter

She walks into the river
with rocks in her pockets,
and the water closes around her
like the arms of a father
saying hello, my lovely one,
hello. How good to see you,
who have been away so long.

The eddying water
tugs at the hem of her dress,
and the small fish gather
to nibble at her ankles, at her knees,
to nibble at her fingers. They will find
it all edible, soon, except
the carnelian ring by which her sister
will identify her.

Bits of paper
float away, the ink now indecipherable.
Was it a note? Notes for another
novel she might have written, something new
to confound the critics? They will cling
to the reeds, will be used
to line ducks' nests, with the down
from their breasts. The water
rises to her shoulders, lifts her hair.

Come, says the river. I have been waiting
for you so long, my daughter.
Dress yourself in my weeds,
let your hair float in my pools,
take on my attributes: fluidity,
the eternal, elemental flow
for which you always longed.
They are found not in words but water.
You will never find them while you breathe,
not in the world of air.

And she opens her mouth
one final time, saying father,
I am here.

Goblin Song

In the bright May-time,
when green herbs are springing,
our hearts they are ringing
like bells in a tower.

We dance as do maidens
upon the cropped hillside
when wedding the bride
unto chivalry's flower,

We prance as do fawnlets
all lissome and amber
and plash in the river
and play by its side,

we sway like the willows
that spring by the water
or maidens with laughter
saluting the bride.

Out, creepings, out, crawlings,
come into the May-light
from out of your night
underneath the high hill,

come dance on the grasses,
like maidens, like fawnlets,
disporting grotesques
celebrating our fill,

with knob-knees and horn-nubs,
pug-noses and tails,
with moss-covered nails,
we crouch and we cower,

in the bright May-time
when green herbs are springing
and our hearts are ringing
like bells in a tower.

Molly

The green of the valley was ringing, was ringing,
and we were lamenting the coming of day
when through the damp grasses, with bare ankles flashing,
our Molly was journeying far and away.

Her kerchief was knotted so not a curl showing
would dance on the breezes that tended to west,
and we were all moaning the going of Molly,
the lily-white prancer, the hyacinth-tressed.

That ringing, that ringing, was calling us churchward
where we owed our morning allegiance to God,
but we were all kneeling beside the old goat-shed
to Molly, whose toes sank into the wet sod.

Molly, my love, you are barred from the village,
your hazelnut eyes are not welcome in school,
and you are condemned to bed down in the stable
beside John the cart-horse and Jimmy the fool,

but the gleam of your legs once led us to the forest
where weasels slid by us and owls spread their wings
with a rushing of feathers, and wild waters bathed us,
so here I am kneeling, while on the bell rings.

Go back to your people, who live beneath branches
that rise like cathedrals in Dublin, and wear
oak leaves stitched together with thorns of the musk-rose,
who place lightning-beetles by night in their hair.

Away you are turning, my Molly, my dear one,
and smilingly crossing our boundary streams,
but when the moon rises I'll see your hand whitely
inviting us into the forest of dreams.

The Goblins

I have frequented the ways, even the byways of men,
I have gone forth silently, still-countenanced and cold;
they have not noticed clustered at my hem
the tattered-earned smirking little goblins bold.

I have bowed and seemed to smile and seemed to converse with them,
while my face remained pale and my words retained their chill,
and the little goblins chattered and clattered at my hem
in voices triumphant and shrill.

Where She Once Lived

This is a place I love; the lawns are clipped,
the yew-hedges like shadowy green walls,
the beds stone-edged and elegantly shaped,
and avenues of birches, leafy halls
where minstrel-birds sing measured madrigals.

A sheet of water slumbers under flags
that raise their yellow standards to the noon,
stately and straight, robed in heraldic rags,
and all the garden seems as in a swoon,
and in the shallows now the small frogs croon.

This is a place I love; the old stone house
with billowing breezy curtains, winding stairs
so silent one can hear the scampering mouse.
Where she once lived now live the pleasant airs;
we feel them come with tears, but happy tears.

The Church of the Forsythia

I dreamed that I wandered through the branches of forsythia
like cathedral arches.
Around me the yellow petals fluttered and blazed
as fire upon torches,
and a dim green silence presided underneath
those solemn branches.

The soil beneath my penitential feet was cold, like stone pavement
swept by chill spring. But on the wind the fluting
hymn of a celebrant,
which may have been a thrush, rose. Oh my heart, crying
now for contentment,

go to the high halls of the forsythia, where the sunlight
filtering through windows
steps in procession with the cowled
praying green shadows,
and listen . . . for the wind in the branches praises
Her in spiraling cantos.

Guenivere in Prison

She clasped her hands, and she unclasped her hands.
She stood up, and she sat back down again.
She sighed and pushed back copper-colored strands
of hair, and sighed and listened to the rain.
The windows were barred; she stood and looked outside
between the bars, and saw the wet gray walls,
and watched a lone bedraggled pigeon stride
the battlements, and trickling waterfalls
form from the turrets. The banners hung soaked and limp.
She set her white hands on the windowsill
and left them until they were cold and damp.
She closed her eyes. And then that pigeon stole,
boldly, while she snatched a somewhat rest,
two strands to make a copper-colored nest.

The Phantom Lover

The one I have loved is a shadow
or the ghost of a dream,
a phantom made of starlight
cast on a stream,
whose voice is the murmur of beeches,
whose touch the wing
of a moth that rises with darkness,
or a spider's sting.

He walks with the sound of branches
that creak in the dark.
I wake and find on my shoulder
a burning mark,
as though hot wax has fallen
on my white skin.
I am conscious of confusion
and pleasing sin.

No boot has come over the casement
though the window's wide,
and only the call of an owl
is sounding outside,
but my love has been, like a shadow
or the ghost of a dream,
a phantom made of starlight
cast on a stream.

Morning Song

Let us away.
The break of day
should find us gone,
and in our stead
an empty bed
shall greet the dawn.

Meanwhile we'll be
beneath a tree
where woodbine twines,
upon the grass
as wild deer pass
through swaying vines.

Beside a stream
we'll talk and dream,
and as it flows,
a scent will come
to make us dumb
from the wild rose.

A wreath of green
to crown a queen
you'll weave for me,
a ring complete
of woodbine sweet
pulled from the tree.

I'll fill your hands
with arching wands
of wild rose sprays
that bloom, like love,
in scented groves
on summer days.

Nor maids nor men
where we'll walk then,
only things wild:
the stream and tree,
and wandering we,
and deer so mild,
all reconciled.

Songs for Ophelia

Echo and Narcissus

Echo calls from the hillside.
Narcissus is there,
and she plaits white-flowering clover
into his hair.

The place where he lies is a tangle
of elder, and vines
of honeysuckle dangle
as he reclines.

The pool is deep that he watches,
and small fishes dart,
while Echo brushes the crickets
from his rags of shirt.

I saw them there one morning,
I and a deer:
his indescribable beauty,
her constant care.

She echoed the sounds of the crickets
(what could she say?),
and he burned in his singular beauty
on the common day.

Paris, the Shepherd

What lies beneath the hawthorn hedges there?
It is Paris, the shepherd, and beside him sleeping
lies Iolanthe on the pillow of his hair,
gold curls that glimmer through the grasses, creeping
like little yellow snakes. Iolanthe, lie still,
sleep, Iolanthe, sleep and continue sleeping;
to waken now is to awake to ill,
to pale, sick cheeks and red eyes blotched with weeping.
For now the pretty Paris opens his eyes,
vain as a jay, the ruddy blue-eyed boy,
to see three goddesses against the skies,
regarding him with mitigated joy.
And now begin Andromache's mad cries,
and crumble now the red-brick walls of Troy.

Falling Boy

The pale boy fell, and as he fell his hair
fanned out and caught a few last rays of light,
shining like copper on a shelf of air.
He crossed the threshold into endless night.
The glimmer of it dulled, as though with wear.

His limbs were bare and awkward in the void;
they scattered like the legs of spiders dropped
without a skein to keep the body buoyed,
or stems of lilies that have just been lopped.
He looked like something recently destroyed.

The shattered wings, that could not break his fall,
left soft white pinions fluttering in space.
His blankened eyes could scarcely now recall
the forfeited proximity of grace,
or love, whose fierce necessities appall.

Theodora Goss

Vivian to Merlin

I called you, and you would not answer me.
What power was it that trapped you in the oak?
They blame me, saying I have cast a spell,
but even if I had that sort of knowledge,
I would not hold you.

When I was young, a girl in Lyonesse,
a prince's daughter running through the fields,
where all the peasants greeted me, or forests,
where I could call the birds down from their nests,
my two braids swinging,

I found a wounded raven, lifted him,
carried him back into my father's castle,
placed him inside a basket on the hay
I'd stolen from the horses. There he sat,
regarding me

with his black eyes, eating the worms and insects
I brought him. And eventually the wing,
which had been wounded by a dog perhaps,
holding the raven in its mouth, was healed.
At first he flew

around my room and perched upon the chest,
the windowsill. You know this story ends
the day he flung himself into the air
and flew over the fields, back to his forest.
Its moral is

you can't hold what you love. Not for a moment,
not for a century. It must have been
another magician, as powerful as yourself,
or a giant who just happened to have a curse
handy. It must have.

I sit here with my back against the oak,
hoping it was a curse and not your choice.
(But who could trap Merlin himself? I could not,
despite the magic you have taught me.) Love,
if you can hear me,

as you sit curled inside the oak tree's bole,
just tell me this: that it was not by choice
you left me, weary of our days and nights,
by daylight casting spells, by night lying
entwined, together.

You can't hold what you love. I would not hold you –
but I had hoped that you would choose, yourself,
to stay with me. And yet you sit there, curled
in silence, Merlin of the silver tongue,
and I wait, hoping . . .

Theodora Goss

April

April has come, like a girl gathering lilacs
in her basket, her arms aching from the heavy
basket filled with the purple and white and lavender
heads of lilacs, beaded with water,
and a bee buzzing around her, thinking
that she is some sort of walking
two-legged bush. Her arms
aching, her feet bare in the wet grass,
the hem of her dress wet.
Carrying a basket full of lilacs
to her mother, and despite the ache
in her arms, laughing
to herself without making a sound,
exultant in the early
morning, thinking to herself, "Mother,
Mother, here they are!"

II. *Summer Songs*

Beauty to the Beast

When I dare walk in fields, barefoot and tender,
trace thorns with my finger, swallow amber,
crawl into the badger's chamber, comb
lightning's loose hair in a crashing storm,
walk in a wolf's eye, lie
naked on granite, ignore the curse
on the castle door, drive a tooth into the boar's hide,
ride adders, tangle the horned horse,
when I dare watch the east
with unprotected eyes, then I dare love you, Beast.

Theodora Goss

Song of the Lady in the Corn

Cornflowers bloom in the borders,
poppies suffuse the field.
He expected resistance,
I was accustomed to yield.

The rough straw clung between us,
the fragrant hay our couch,
and he was a rugged farm-boy,
and I was a lady smooth.

Come into my household,
awkward handsome boy.
The badgers walk in the trenches,
the delicate deer slip by.

The rowan offers her berries
freely, eaglets wail.
The wild woods hymn together.
Come live in rain and hail,

where bears pad through the forests,
and rivers deeply glide
through cavernous embankments
carved out from mountainside,

where we shall live in regions
shadowy and chill,
and dance with crooked creatures
come from beneath the hill,

and you shall cry a-mornings
For your mother and your bed,
and can no more return to them
than wake the dead.

Advice to a Daughter

The moon's the mistress for you: bind up your long brown hair,
and enter into her workshop, and learn her dark technique.
Learn to alter and falter and fatten, week to week;
learn to glide without turning, and silently stare and stare.

Learn her blank luminescence, and learn to daily draw
the seas of all the world without need of net or sieve,
to trail upon their waters one negligent white sleeve
and confound the bearded sages with inimitable law.

The Forest Pool

There is a secret place within these woods
(the oaks know of it but will never tell),
a pool so set about with ancient trees
that daylight never troubles its green depths.
There live strange fish, and something stranger yet
than any fish. A boy came on it once,
an ordinary boy, a woodsman's son,
who, late for school, decided he would try
a shorter way, the woods being known to him,
but somehow in his hurry missed the path
and came where no one comes. He stood amazed,
so still and green it was beneath the trees
and on the surface of the pool itself –
you would have thought a breeze could never come
to trouble its placidity. He knelt,
wanting a better look (being curious,
the sort of boy who's always good at sums).
At first he only saw his sunburnt face
turned brownish-green, his tangled yellow hair
turned greenish too as though he had become
another boy who lived within the pool,
himself and not himself. And then he saw,
deep in the pool, a something – a dim shape
that rose and rose – a fish – no, not a fish,
but glittering just as though it were a fish.
He could not make it out until at last
it broke the surface. There, it was – a hand.
But what a hand, the skin as white as stone,

covered with overlapping silver scales
along the back and to the finger joints.
And then a head, as white and just as scaled,
with eyes as green as was the pool itself,
a flatish nose above a smiling mouth,
white neck and shoulders slick with waterdrops,
white breasts – and here he blushed. How delicate
her ears were as they curved into her cheek,
her collarbones that spread like silver wings,
her breasts – he blushed again and looked away,
but felt her fingers touch his sunburnt hand,
pleasantly cold, and looked at her again.
She smiled and drew him to her, just as though
she wished to whisper something in his ear,
perhaps the secret of the forest pool,
the story of her origin and name.
Too late he saw them, sharp and white as stone,
moist with her spit – a double row of teeth.
There is no more. The story is told out.
But if you were to go into the woods,
to lose yourself and find a forest pool,
beside its still green depths you'd see his bones,
turned greenish now with lichens and with moss.
I tell you that I do not know the way
(the oaks know, but will surely never tell).

The Stones by the Stream

Over the stones by the stream a spreading lichen
has formed itself into unreadable runes,
and the stream itself flows beneath the ancient oak-trees
intoning unknown tunes.

She woke in the dim brown light beneath their branches,
stretching her supple fingers and gripping the stones
with toes that were mottled, as though with patterns of lichen,
and had too many bones.

She crouched by the stones and dipped her astonishing fingers
into the stream, where they hung like lanky weeds,
but the guppies darted away and mocked her hunger
with lines of popping beads.

He walked through the forest, an axe slung over his shoulder,
whistling a tune he had heard at the village fair.
He grinned when he saw her, bare like a woman bathing,
and switched to a bawdier air.

His bones are scattered beside the roots of an oak tree
like syllables of a language learned in a dream,
as unreadable as the spreading runes of the lichen
that have covered the stones by the stream.

Theodora Goss

The Ophelia Cantos

I.

Lilies tangle in her hair: green stems
like water-snakes.

II.

                           A disembodied hand
floats on the surface. So much has been lost
already: toes, the lobe of her left ear.
But this remains, a damp, immaculate
sign, like a message saved from the dark current.

III.

She wandered through the courtyard in her tattered
dress distributing wild violets.
She called us whores – your son ma'am, not your husband's
I think – and knaves – the taxes sir, your cellar
is stocked with sweet Moselle. We called this madness.

IV.

Indicia of her innocence: to be
a maiden floating dead among the flowers.

V.

She will become an elegant and mute
image: the sodden velvet coat, the sinking
coronet of poppies, virgin's bower,
and eglantine. The replicable girl.

(A blob of Chinese white becomes a hand.
The artist puts his brush in turpentine,
the model pulls her stockings on.)

VI.

                    And yet,
surrounded by the water-lily stems,
her face appears an enigmatic mask:
a drowned Medusa in her snaking hair.
The lilies gape around her like pink mouths,
telling us nothing we can understand.

VII.

Her eyes stare upward: dead and not quite dead.

The Marshes

The marshes call,
the marshes so wild,
all yellow under the moon,
and the small green frogs
raise their heads from the slime
to croak a beckoning tune.

The marshes call
with a sibilant voice,
the hiss of settling mire,
and they whisper a promise
that is no promise,
a negative heart's desire.

I answer, alone
while the moon shines on me,
insisting I will not come,
but the night wears away,
and the brain grows weary,
and the heart goes numb.

The Beckoner

She rises at night with her robes all around her,
rises just like you rise from sleep,
in a fairness of heavy unbound tresses
so rich they could make you weep.

The moon is a pale and horrified witness,
the cypresses moan as they sway in the dark,
and even the grasses lament in whispers
as she surveys the park.

Then she is away, and soon we will see her
reaching her hand like an alba rose
to tap, so lightly, upon our window,
holding an elegant pose.

Beauty is deadly – how well we know it –
her cheeks have a treacherous living stain,
and we will kiss them, and come to her beckoning,
and never return again.

The Gypsy's Warning

This ground is cursed. I would leave it,
if I were a man, as you are:
leave the moss-overgrown
stones that bound the estate,
leave the damp of the hollow,
leave the hill where a scar
reminds you that penance is needed,
even if proffered late.

You will not listen to me,
to the gypsy with rain in the tangles
of hair escaping her kerchief
who watches with answerless eyes.
You ride, young lord, through the shadows
of immemorial beeches:
all yours, all yours, but I'd leave them,
young lord, if you were wise.

Ride to the white mausoleum
where your ancestors wait to receive you,
ride past the marshy expanses
where frogs make ominous sounds,
ride past the ruined hillside
without a notion of pity,
without remorse, to the manor,
satisfied with your rounds.

The tree that stood on that hillside
was older than this structure,
older than your rights here
or your family's name.
All your ancestors shivered
at the fall of that timber,
whose trunk is hewn for a pleasure-house,
whose branches roast your game.

Go to the church with the steeple
and sleep among downy pillows;
the gods that are older than boundaries
are opening up their eyes.
They meet in the damp of the hollow,
they dance on the marshy expanses
where their feet make no dint on the turf
and the air seems filled with sighs.
You would leave, young lord, you would leave here,
if you, like me, were wise.

Three Swans

A mist lay on the surface of the lake.
We seemed to swim in air
beneath that pre-dawn lemon-yellow light,
our bodies bare

and chilled within the boundaryless domain
where haze and water meet,
our fingers wrinkled, each of our toes numb,
and our hair wet.

The sun had climbed an intervening hill
and when at last it came
to the summit, it sent forth a single flare
like liquid flame.

Then suddenly the mist which had enclosed
us in a scattered glow,
a nimbus like the halo of a saint,
began to go.

And as the haze dried off we saw upon
the surface of the lake,
three swans, like tufts of white among the reeds,
barely awake.

Each swan had tucked a leg into its wing
and from its ankle shone,
on orange skin, a ring of antique gold
carved with a crown.

From each such ring depended a slim chain
linking it to another,
so that the three were inextricably
harnessed together.

We watched those white swans arch their supple necks
and felt their black eyes glare
as they rose from the surface of the lake, the maimed and lovely
Children of Lir.

By Tidal Pools

At first she watched in case he should return,
by tidal pools where iridescent snails,
tyrian and cochineal, crawled about,
saltwater glistening on their subtle shells.

"He was like you," she'd whisper, kneeling down,
one knee, and then another, on wet rock.
"Like you he wore his house upon his back,
carrying Ithaca." She would lean out

over a tidal pool's now-shadowed depths
and see, below, the snails, their shells gone dull,
above them her reflection, dull as well.
Eventually her knees would cramp and ache.

She'd stand and each ridged whorl would glow again,
a demonstration of the dyer's art.
Where she had knelt, her dress clung to her shins.
She'd whisper then, "Does he lie on some shore

where snails leave glistening tracks upon his eyes,
or has he found his home?" She'd turn and walk
over the rocks while wavelets lapped her feet,
wondering when the sea had grown so cold.

Helen in Sparta

Helen is wandering, sunburnt, angry,
along a road by a dusty hill,
tripping over the rocks from a quarry,
vaguely shrill.

The dust hangs about that hill like a nimbus,
dust from marble, chalky-white,
catching and milkily dispersing
the Attic light.

The quarry looks like a giant's staircase,
with blocky cuttings descending down
into a glaring cavity – she,
with rags for gown,

rags that resemble antique linen,
hums and mutters and claws at her face,
browned and withered, with white hair streaming
and a kind of grace.

She clambers up a dusty incline
and suddenly turns to stand quite still,
a mad white deity overlooking
the quarry hill.

The Bells

I heard them peal, the bells within my brain,
and watched the white waves crashing on the shore,
and never asked (I could have asked) for more
than these – the salted air, the clanging pain.
I walked the beaches where dark caverns stared
out from the cliff-face glaring to the west,
and never stopped (I could have stopped) for rest,
and nothing seemed to matter – how I fared,
how the damp rags were hanging on my frame,
how the green sea-scum dangled from each tress.
I listened to the bells of Lyonesse
and found, upon those sands, nothing to change or blame.

Songs for Ophelia

An Education

I was sent to school with witches,
and I learned the spells they speak
in a sharp gray mouse's squeak
while making nine black stitches.

For their spells require small things:
the voice of the mouse, and a line
of hyphens in black twine
(oh, the might in colored strings),

drops that the lilies weep
when we shake them after dawn,
bits of cambric, bits of lawn,
and a doll's eyes closed in sleep.

And it does not matter now
that our spells do petty things,
that they prick like hornets' stings,
that they cannot scare a crow,

for the principle's the same:
when we exorcize your moles
with our pretty rigmaroles
(which you think a charming game),

we remember other times,
when we rode the wings of the moon
and the stars rehearsed a tune
with consequential rhymes.

The Witch-Wife

Light the fire, sweetheart. I am cold,
cold and wet to the skin.
I have been chasing, over hill and dale,
a ewe that heard a wild dog wail
and would not come in.

Then why are you wearing dancing-slippers,
spotted with clay?

I heard a wind in the willows,
tossing them all day,
so I dreamed that I was dancing
like the trees, and began prancing
about the house, in play.

And why are flowers tucked into the waistband
of your dress, my sweet?

I passed a patch of poppies
while walking in the wheat
and took the scarlet to adorn me.
Surely, love, you cannot scorn me,
looking so neat?

You are lovely, but the golden ringlets of your hair
are tangled and wild.

Did I not tell? I met in the meadow
an enchanting child,
who caught her hands in my tresses
while giving me soft caresses
that soothed and beguiled.

You answer calmly, my dear, but your eyes
are strangely aglow.

And what is there in that?
A moment ago
I saw your face in the glass,
and think me a lucky lass
to have caught such a fellow.

He lit the fire and went out
to pen the ewe
while the flames changed the white of her cheek
to a ruddy hue.
Then she rose and put on a cauldron,
and when he appeared
he wondered at the vigor
with which she stirred and stirred.

Fairy Tale

You ask where you will find her. Beside the singing fountains,
where orange trees are blossoming and perfuming the air;
where night is like an orchard, with orange blossoms shining,
and the spirit of the fountains unbinds its wild blue hair.

Ask courage of the clockwork bird and follow where it tells you,
the talking bird that maps the long brown road to heart's desire.
Pass by the groaning forests, and boars that speak in parables,
and stop your ears as you approach the taunting realms of fire.

When you have reached the final citadel, you'll find the trousers
that give a man a league at step, the zither that is wise
enough to know how you can open all the cut-glass doorways.
Release the cat that smiles and blinks its dreaming amber eyes.

Then, after chasm and abyss, and after crystal mountains
that dazzle and confuse the mind like vertical green seas,
you'll come at last beneath the trees of fragrant orange-orchards
where the princess in the singing fountains bathes her soft white knees.

I Knew a Woman

I knew a woman kind as any star.
She wrapped the night wind warm about her neck.
She sang like crickets chirping in a jar.
She called the violet twilight her true home
and dusted constellations. For her sake
the moon swept out its pewter-powdered dome.

Black clouds would scorn to sail on common ponds
and light upon the liquid of her mind.
They flared and ruffed their fluted wings like swans.
And when she spoke the poplars strove to hear,
and when sometimes she cried out in the wind,
her voice was more than all the stars could bear.

Green Man

Come to me out of the forest, man of leaves,
whose arms are branches, whose legs are two trunks,
rough bark covered with lichen. Come and take
my hands in yours, and lead me in this dance:

In spring, green buds will sprout upon your head;
in summer they will lengthen into leaves.
Oak man, willow man, linden man, which are you?
In autumn, they will fall, and through the winter
you will be bare, with only clumps of snow
or birds upon your branches.

Come and love me,
my man of leaves, my forest man. For you,
I'll be an alder woman, birch woman.
In spring I'll wear pink blossoms like the cherry;
in summer ripening fruit will bend my boughs;
in autumn I will bear, distributing
a hundred seeds, our children. And the birds
will sing my praises. Let us learn to love
the sun and wind together; let us twine
our bodies, filled with sap, until we make
a single tree on which two different kinds
of leaves are growing, where birds build their nests,
among whose roots the squirrels hide their nuts,
storing them for winter.

A hundred years from now, we will still stand,
crooked perhaps, the sap running more slowly,
our two hearts beating, separately and together,
under the summer skies, in autumn rains.

The Gentleman

Has the milk gone sour this morning?
Are there tracks upon the floor
where you could have sworn you swept
carefully the night before?
Are the window shutters open?
Did the clock forget to chime?
Could you simply have forgotten
to set the time? Surely not.

Are the chickens agitated?
Could a fox have come last night
and sniffed around their coop,
to put them in a fright?
There's a fox that walks on two legs;
when he comes, the farmyard dog
pricks his ears and sits as silent
as a log. Unfortunately.

Is the horse's mane completely
in a tangle, and its hide
crusted with the mud that splashed
from its hooves during the ride?
That's how you know. The Gentleman
does love his nightly ride. And the maid
milking the cows this morning smiles
mysteriously. Oh, for goodness' sake.

You should do something. Gather
the town together, determine to catch
the malefactor. How many of you
have had your tulips trampled,
your best cow addled, your daughter
suddenly dreamy? But. What
if he were brought to justice,
black boots in the courtroom,
black eyes laughing at you,
at the good wives, industrious,
neat as a pin in their cotton
gowns, making you feel,
well, ridiculous, and somehow flushed,

and worse, what if the cabbages
bolted, and the asparagus flopped,
and the squash were all infested
with worms. You can't trust him.
And worse yet, what if the moon
refused to change, and the leaves
on the trees never caught the fire
of autumn. And it was your fault.

I tell you, my dear:

If the milk was sour this morning,
and the laundry is in knots,
if the geraniums are missing
from their flowerpots,
if the mice have gotten into
the bacon and the cheese,
laugh and let the Gentleman do
as he pleases. I know, what a mess.

But a robin's on the handle
of the shovel, singing softly,
and the clouds are floating overhead.
Admit, the world is mostly
as it ought to be. Tonight the moon
will pull the distant tide,
and the Gentleman will come to take
his nightly ride. With a kiss for you

even if you don't notice.
But my dear,
you do.

Foxes

Deep in the ferns they are creeping, their sweeping
tails setting swaying the ferns as they crawl,
little red foxes, an army of redcoats,
elegant-eared and cunningly small,
like rubies half-hid by a billowing shawl.
Deep in the ferns underneath the green forest,
on slender white ankles, with button-black eyes,
they swarm, and we catch just a glimpse in the half-light,
and hear through the thicket the witty wild cries
of those delicate, flashing, sanguineous spies.

III. *Autumn Songs*

Autumn, the Fool

The leaves float on the water like patches of motley.
Autumn, the fool, has dropped them into the lake,
where they rival the costume, not of the staid brown duck,
but the splendid drake.

He capers down the lanes in his ragged garments,
a comical figure shedding last year's leaves,
but as he passes the crickets begin their wailing
and the chipmunk grieves.

The willow bends down to watch herself in the water
and shivers at the sight of her yellow hair.
Autumn the fool has passed her, and soon her branches
will be bare.

Nymphs Finding the Head of Orpheus

The water has a dim and glassy hue.
A mass of airy bubbles clings to curls
that tumble through the river-bottom's marls,
and cypresses hang heavy with their woe.

Our hair-tips touch the water's urgent tow
as we lift this possessor of blue lips
and single eye that out its substance weeps,
from the dark river bound by thorny may.

Now sing, my sisters, piercingly and slow,
and sweetly as the honey of the comb,
for this rank weed, and beat the hollow drum,
and kiss and turn the leprous cheeks away.

What Her Mother Said

Go, my child, through the forest
to your grandmother's house, in a glade
where poppies with red mouths grow.

In this basket is an egg laid
three days ago,
the three days our Lord lay sleeping,
unspotted, from a white hen.
In this basket is also a skein
of wool, without stain,
unspun. And a comb that the bees
industriously filled
from the clover in the far pasture,
unmown since the sun
thawed it, last spring.

If you can take it without breaking
anything, I will give you
this ring.

Stay, child, and I'll give you this cap
to wear, so the forest creatures whose eyes
blink from the undergrowth will be aware
that my love protects you. The creatures
lurking beneath the trees,
weasels and stoats and foxes, and worse
than these.

And child, you must be wise
in the forest.

When the wolf finds you, remember:
be courteous, but evasive. No answer
is better than a foolish one.

If you stray from the path, know
that I strayed also. It is no great matter,
so long as you mark the signs:
where moss grows on bark, where a robin
builds her nest. The sun
sailing west.

But do not stop to gather
the hawthorn flowers, nor yet
the red berries which so resemble
coral beads. They are poisonous.
And do not stop to listen
to the reeds.
He must not be there first,
at your grandmother's house.

When your grandmother serves you,
with a silver spoon, on a dish
like a porcelain moon, Wolf Soup,
remember to say your grace
before you eat.

And know that I am pleased
with you, my child.

But remember, when returning through the forest,
kept warm against the night by a cloak
of the wolf's pelt:
the hunter is also a wolf.

The Changeling

What do you do? He wore his leather jacket to school,
pulled the fire alarm, felt up one of the nuns.
Detention was a time to draw rocket ships
or race cars. He liked things that go fast (skateboards),
things that were secret (cellars), things that squealed
(mice mostly, but also hamsters). He never harmed them
but put them in desks, purses, girls' hair.
He read books on poisonous mushrooms and making bombs.

What do you do? Tell him, you are a doll,
created from sticks and feathers? Go back where
you came from? He would grin, get your daughter pregnant,
set your barn on fire.

The Slopes of Eden

I have forgotten the slopes of Eden:
the gorse that grows there
and the bare gray stones.
I have forgotten the torturous pines
and the piles of white bones.

It was a charred and empty vista,
down to the sea
that roared and moaned,
the image of everything long abandoned,
and razed or ruined.

I have been told there was once a garden
where oranges grew
and the lime flowers swayed,
where hovering birds not as big as your thumb
upset the shade.

I have been told there was once a river
that ran to the ocean,
which laughed on the sand,
and that gazelles with hooves like adamant
came to your hand.

This is not Eden as I have seen it,
not the dry place
that I knew as a child.
Is it a tale, and were the tale-tellers
simply beguiled?

I have forgotten, but I will go back there:
I need to remember
the sting of that spray,
and the sweet smell of gorse on the harsh rocks of Eden,
and the empty day.

As I Was Walking

I met, as I was walking,
Nature, my mother's mother,
beside the cold gray waters
of an undulating sea,

like granite filled with motion,
like silk the hue of gravel,
whose veins of quartz or borders
of lace broke endlessly.

She stared at the horizon
where nothing moved or altered,
while over us a cold wind
rearranged the clouds

that looked like chunks of boulder
hewn in some gray quarry.
A premature white moon slipped
through their scattered crowds.

"Lady," I said, staring
at the far horizon,
wondering why she stood there,
"I have loved you long.

Theodora Goss

"My mother told me stories
of your wild procession,
and when a child she sang me
sleeping with your song."

She neither moved nor answered
for an extended moment.
At last she turned and faced me.
I saw her blank gray eyes,

blind, with a film across them,
like foam upon the shingle.
They could not fix me, scanning
instead the darkened skies.

"Welcome, my daughter's daughter,"
she said with a voice like pebbles
rattling down the slopes
of a long-abandoned mine.

"Recall your mother's stories
of when I danced through forests
with ivy-covered maenads,
drinking golden wine,

"Recall the clashing cymbals,
and still the wild procession
will live within that memory.
But I can stir no more,

"and the only song remaining
is the sound of billows
desolately breaking
on this barren shore."

The moon slipped through the heavens
as we stood together,
watching the horizon
like an empty rune.

Then I took her hands
and danced upon the shingle,
and she sang, like pebbles cracking,
the old, old tune.

One Who Forgot

She sits, the house drawn about her, so silently;
out in the street the lamp lights gleam.
She has been sitting still through the afternoon,
lost in a dream, in a waking dream.

Look at her hair, how it shines in the firelight:
once when her feet were wet with dew,
bare on the chilly green grasses of springtime,
wandering beneath where the wild briar blows,

she was as lithe as a deer in its running,
she was as trilling as slender streams.
Lightly she gamboled through sunlit meadows,
this lady now lost in dreams.

Bent is her head and how bowed her shoulders,
curved are her fingers like necks of swans.
Look in her eyes: you will feel much older.
She, with the visage of drawn-out stone,

once knew the paths through the thicketed forest
that led at the last to You-Know-Where.
One day grown old, she no longer remembered.
Look in her tattered eyes if you dare!

The Ruined Cathedral

Gray monks have wandered here, chanting their canticles,
great kings have walked beneath these archways of wrought stone,
and holy ladies read windows of parables,
and late into the night, possessing all alone
the rose-shaped turrets, bats have dived and shrieked and spun.

The monks are laid to rest beneath the graveyard grass,
the kings beneath grand slabs, the ladies in fine tombs,
and dust and sunlight now are all that shift or pass,
except that little bats still wheel across the rooms,
the final visitants that come, or are to come.

Isolde in the Forest

Isolde walked among the leafless trees.
A month ago, the aspen had been green
and quivering like a maiden at the touch
of her first lover. Then the grove of oaks
had rustled its red leaves like dowagers
whispering gossip, and the stream had run
between moss-covered banks. How they had changed.
The aspen stood, a slender, shaking thing
stripped of her robes. The oaks stirred silently.
The stream now flowed between bare earth and rock.
All had turned gray, and where not gray then brown.
Just like my love for Tristan, she thought, and his
for me. And as she thought and walked and thought,
the chill wind nipping at her fingertips
and her thoughts growing colder than the wind,
high in the oaks a squirrel chirred, and a bird
called from the aspen, and a drop of rain
fell on the stream's blank surface, promising
that spring would come again.

Under the Oaks

Under the oaks, the columbines stand stately,
under the oaks.

Where has she gone, that we played with just lately?
Under the oaks.

Red and yellow the columbines, jesters' caps.
Under the oaks

red leaf rustles, yellow twig snaps. What walks
under the oaks?

Her long red hair, her shroud now yellow, it is she
that walks.

Lucy

Lucy walked into the forest; the moon hung like a scythe
over a harvested landscape, bared by autumn and death,
and above the clouds moved silently with the swiftness of a breath.

She carried a wicker basket filled with necessary things:
a flask of dew, a tortoiseshell comb, a pair of butterfly wings
found on a budding rosebush, mysteriously, last spring.

She walked into a clearing and uttered a low, sweet cry
(I will not tell you the words of it, an ancient lullaby),
and then she stood and waited, and frowned a bit to see.

Then suddenly the Elder began to sway and turn,
and all of that grove of branches similarly to churn,
as though a command had animated the artwork on an urn.

Brown trunks twisted and trembled, roots were pulled from the ground,
thick with the mud of ages, and ivy wreaths unwound,
and the trees stepped from their places, with a snap and a creaking sound.

Now Lucy stands among them, and gives them a smile and a glance;
scattering the last of their leaves, they bow and they advance,
and the Elder invites Lucy to participate in the dance.

The moon hangs over the mountains, curved like a scimitar,
and the clouds have gathered together to cover every star,
and the place where the trees are dancing appears as a long bare scar.

Far off in the towns the men are dreaming in their degrees,
but above the forest the death's-head of the moon sails on and sees
Lucy, laughing and prancing among the dancing trees.

The Chase

The wolves of the night came coursing
over the hills of the chase,
and the stag of the sun, with antlers
of ruddy, beaten gold,
snuffled his delicate nostrils
and turned his slender face,
turned as the wolves came coursing
down the open wold.

The stag of the sun stood a moment
to sniff the westering air,
then he leaped from the meridian's
radiant curvature,
and he left a track, as of amber,
on the waters of the lake,
and he singed the singing grasses
of the valley floor.

The hills were briefly gilded
where the stag of the sun had gone,
then the mountain slopes turned ruddy
while the wold lay dull and dim;
he stood at last on the summit
of the highest mountain peak,
and he stamped one hoof on the icy
stone of the valley's rim.

One final blaze from that stamping
sent a ray into the dusk
that lay on the lake's still waters
and over the silent grass,
and the wolves of the night, in their coursing,
paused for a moment's space,
paused and lifted their faces
to watch him turn and pass.

Then over the peak of the mountain
he passed, and the ruddy ice
that had taken its hue from his standing
on hooves of beaten gold
for the space of a single moment
on the summit of the peak,
turned dark, and the coursing wolves
of the night devoured the wold.

The Genius

If you have met him shining among the cobbles,
that genius whose yowl will frighten the moon,
that werewolf-man, if you have witnessed him at noon
whistling, walking tattered with the natty rabbles,
if you have seen him among bankers and bakers, ragged and shining,
and thought him lucky: every night the night devours him.

A Walk in Autumn

Autumn has come, and the fields are sodden –
wild geese drift on a southward air –
and over the hills the forests are burning
to umber and ashes, everywhere.

I walk outside, on the damp expanses
of broken grass where the horses graze
and bend to inhale from the final roses
that open during these shortened days.

I want to cry on such autumn mornings,
as I cry over Antigone's pain –
for the season's slow, symbolic drama
of a maiden prematurely slain.

Her name was Summer – her hair the grasses,
her gown the forest's leafy cloth,
her chaplet roses, the flock she herded
those geese the wind is carrying south.

She lies unburied, exposed to weather
in tattered garments the worse for wear,
her chaplet scattered, her flock departed,
on shattered remnants of her hair.

But the season resists such allegory,
denying the poetry of loss and death,
insists on the fact – the hills denuded,
a rim of ice on each ragged leaf.

A Day With Rain

We wandered through the house on a day with rain,
down the long hallways searching for explanations,
and listened to the dawn and twilight concatenations
of birds, and followed gray drops down the pane.

The trees shivered in their shawls of lambent drops,
while somewhere in the woods soaked wolves sat glumly,
watching a wet sheen cover the world completely,
and the wind hid, curling into the treetops.

Tonight the moon is an oval pool and the waves
of the leaves of the poplars ruffle;
all day we have waited through the silent scuffle,
and tonight her spirit hunches with the damp wolves.

The Witch

Sometimes in the morning, the mist curled into the corners
of the house like a cat, and Grimalkin, she would cry,
come to me, my Grimalkin. She would gather
the mist to her, and stroke it, and it would settle
in her lap, and lick itself.

                                Sometimes, she wove
cobwebs and out of the cloth, thin, gray, luminescent,
she would cut the pattern for a dress. But for what purpose?
Where could she wear it? Where could she go, except
to the pond, where she would kneel and dip her fingers
into the water, and stir, and out would jump
a trout, thick, silver, luminescent, and splashing
water onto her dress, whose hem was already
soaked and covered with mud.

                                She would make it speak,
recite Shakespearean sonnets, sing old songs,
before she put it into the pot. Witches
are lonely, but also hungry, and practical
in their impracticality. She had learned
how from her mother, the old witch, now dead
if witches are ever entirely dead, which is doubtful.

She never wondered who her father had been,
a peasant gathering wood, perhaps a hunter,
perhaps even a prince, on his way to the country
where a princess had been promised for dispatching
a dragon or something similar, and had seen
a light through the trees, and found her mother waiting,
and perhaps gone on the next morning, and perhaps not.

Her mother had built the house by the edge of the pond,
out of gray stone and branches of white birch,
birds' nests and moss, and spit to hold it together.
That is how witches build what they call houses.
What they are not: sturdy, comfortable.
What they are: cold.

                              There was still a row of bottles
in the cupboard, holding martens' eyes, dried frogs,
robins' eggs, random feathers, balls of string,
oak galls. She had forgotten what they were for.
From the rafters hung a fox's skeleton.

Once, village girls had come to visit her mother
for charms to attract the schoolmaster's attention,
make their rivals' hair fall out, abortions.

Afterward, they would say, Did you see her? Standing
by the door? In her ragged dress, with her tangled hair,
I tell you, she creeps me out. But they stopped coming
after the old witch disappeared and her daughter
was left alone. Sometimes she would remember
the smell of the bread in their pockets, the clink of coins,
their dresses covered with embroidery,
their whispering, and look at her reflection
in the pond, floating on the water like a ghost.

Sometimes she made the frogs at the edge of the pond,
calling to one another, speak to her.
"Pretty one," they would say, "in your spider silk,
in your birchbark shoes, like a princess lost in the woods,
kiss us." But she knew that was not her story.

Sometimes she would make the birds perch on her fingers
and sing to her: warblers, thrushes, chickadees,
and sing to them out of tune, then break their necks
and roast them.

Sometimes she would gather the stones
that had fallen from her house, and think of making
a dog, a stone dog. Then, she would forget.
It was the forgetting that made her what she was,
her mother's daughter. Witches never remember
important things: that fire burns, and that bottles
labeled poison are not to be drunk. Witches
are always doing what they should not, dancing
at midnight with the Gentleman, kicking their skirts
over the tops of their stockings, kissing frogs
they know perfectly well won't turn into princes.

She makes no magic. Although the stories won't tell you,
witches are magic. They do not need the props
of a magician, the costumes or the cards,
the scarves, the rabbits. They came down from the moon
originally, and it still calls to them,
so they go out at night, when the moon is shining,
and make no magic, but magic happens around them.

Sometimes at night she would look up at the moon
and call Mother? Mother? but never got an answer.

I want you to imagine: her ragged dress,
her hair like cobwebs, her luminescent eyes,
mad as all witches are, stirring the pond
like a cauldron (witches need no cauldrons, whatever
the stories tell you) while above her the clouds
are roiling and a storm is about to gather.

Autumn's Song

You are not alone.

If they could, the oaks would bend down to take your hands,
bowing and saying, Lady, come dance with us.
The elder bushes would offer their berries to hang
from your ears or around your neck.
The wild clematis known as Traveler's Joy
would give you its star-shaped blossoms for your crown.
And the maples would offer their leaves,
russet and amber and gold,
for your ball gown.

The wild geese flying south would call to you, Lady,
we will tell your sister, Summer, that you are well.
You would reply, *Yes, bring her this news –*
the world is old, old, yet we have friends.
The squirrels gathering nuts, the garnet hips
of the wild roses, the birches with their white bark.

You would dress yourself in mist and early frost
to tread the autumn dances – the dance of fire
and fallen leaves, the expectation of snow.
And when your sister Winter pays a visit,
You would give her tea in a ceramic cup,
bread and honey on a wooden plate.

You would nod, as women do, and tell each other,
The world is more magical than we know.

You are not alone.

Listen: the pines are whispering their love,
and the sky herself, gray and low, bends down
to kiss you on both cheeks. *Daughter, she says,
I am always with you. Listen: my winds are singing
autumn's song.*

Shoes of Bark

What would you think
if I told you that I was beautiful?
That I walked through the orchards in a white cotton dress,
wearing shoes of bark.

In early morning, when mist lingered over the grass,
and the apples, red and gold, were furred with dew,
I picked one, biting into its crisp, moist flesh,
then spread my arms and looked up at the clouds,
floating high above, and the clouds looked back at me.
By the edge of a pasture I opened milkweed pods,
watching the white fluff float away on the wind.

I held up my dress and danced among the chickory
under the horses' mild, incurious gaze
and followed the stream along its meandering ways.

What would you think
if I told you that I was magical?
That I had russet hair down to the backs of my knees
and the birds stole it for their nests
because it was stronger than horsehair and softer than down.
That when the storm winds roiled,
I could still them with a word.

That when I called, the gray geese would call back
come with us, sister, and I considered rising
on my own wings and following them south.

But if not me, who would make the winter come?
Who would breathe on the windows, creating landscapes of frost,
and hang icicles from the gutters?

What would you think, daughter, if I told you
that in a dress of white wool and deerhide boots
I danced the winter in? And that in spring,
dressed in white cotton lawn, wearing birchbark shoes,
I wandered among the deer and marked their fawns
with my fingertips? That I slept among the ferns?

Would you say, she is old, her mind is wandering?
Or would you say, I am beautiful, I am magical,
and go yourself to dance the seasons in?

(Look in my closet. You will find my shoes of bark.)

The Frost

The frost came on the harvest,
and fallow flowed the air;
the sheaves cleaved off in earnest
and all the skies grew bare.

The clouds fled off and blankness
arrayed the atmosphere,
and autumn in her fastness
had not one cloth to wear.

The leaves betrayed the branches
and grasses hueless hung
upon the valley's haunches,
the hueless weeds among,

and over all that landscape
the season turned,
while swallows made escape
and the berries burned.

Theodora Goss

Chrysanthemums

These are the ragged flowers
present at every gravesite.

Imagine a cloud of petals
like a ruffled cockatoo,
like a slice of wedding cake
with the narrow end eaten,
a pile of lace with leaves
as tough as a toad's skin,
smelling of aniseed.
We give these to the dead.

As they go into the darkness,
the heads of chrysanthemums
must light their way, like lamps.

IV. *Winter Songs*

The Snow

Listen: The snow is falling
with a whisper to the ground,
and it settles on the grasses
like a cold white shawl.

What do you think it whispers?
Just such a silent sound
as white cats make when passing
with white footfall.

The Bear's Daughter

She dreams of the south. Wandering through the silent castle,
where snow has covered the parapets and the windows
are covered with frost, like panes of isinglass,
she dreams of pomegranates and olive trees.

But to be the bear's daughter is to be a daughter, as well,
of the north. To have forgotten a time before
the tips of her fingers were blue, before her veins
were blue like rivers flowing through fields of ice.

To have forgotten a time before her boots
were elk-leather lined with ermine.

Somewhere in the silent castle, her mother is sleeping
in the bear's embrace, and breathing pomegranates
into his fur. She is a daughter of the south,
with hair like honey and skin like orange-flowers.

She is a nightingale's song in the olive groves.

And her daughter, wandering through the empty garden,
where the branches of yew trees rubbing against each other
sound like broken violins,

dreams of the south while a cold wind sways the privet,
takes off her gloves, which are lined with ermine, and places
her hands on the rim of the fountain, in which the sun
has scattered its colors, like roses trapped in ice.

Our Lady of the Nightmoths

When, one night, the nightmoths came,
powdered wings against her skin,
she lay down and closed her eyes,
slept and dreamed, and went with them.

Clutching tresses of her hair,
furred and squeaking like a mouse,
spread like parachutes in air,
they went any wind to north.

Nightmoths squealed behind her ears,
rubbed against her elbow joints.
She flew over valleys where
artist earth with icebergs paints.

She flew over mountains where
wolves elope with hungry ease,
where the caribou prepare
merger with the antlered trees.

Soon the nightmoths brought her north,
to the land where snows respire,
where each night the sky consumes
itself in multicolored fire.

Theodora Goss

There they settled her to wait
while her hair grew white like glass,
where the snow's white termites bit
through her legs and diamond grass

sprouted from her cheeks and chin.
She had waited half a year
when the Nightmoth Lady came,
winging steady through the clear,

dropping powder from her membranes,
clouded in the nightmoth swarm.
Furred antennae felt the cold maid,
slender feelers closed and made her warm.

Songs for Ophelia

The Mountains of Never

I went to the mountains of Never, which flourish their peaks for the moon,
white as the wrist of a lady, white as a fountain of may,
and the journey lasted forever, although it was over too soon,
for the mountains of Never are nearer, and farther, than away.

At the mountains I met a lady whose wrist was as white as the snows,
who sat with her white face lifted, blankened and blind, to the east;
I sat and watched her eyelids as a thousand moons arose,
and slowly the snows on her shoulders, flake by flake, increased.

Finally, over her face, there was only a hillock of white,
the white of the mountains of Never, that flourish their peaks for the moon.
So I turned to the hills and valleys that ranged beyond my sight
and sat with my white face lifted, still, and still, as stone.

Winter Scene

In a country of snow,
the pines shiver and from their narrowness let fall
the snow like doves. Upon gray twilight call
the winds, so bitterly, moaning low.

Dim snowflakes dance
about a silent steeple. Threads of stars
begin, as swiftly night her violet arras
weaves, to glimmer. Eyes of owls, entrancing,

in hushed cold
survey the hills where prey in niches hide.
Lovely death on frosted pinions glides
between the bent yews old.

The Valley of the Elves

In the valley of the Elves,
where the Elven men reside,
lives a maiden tall as poplars
and like a snow-bank fair,
whose plaintive voice resembles
the murmuring of tides,
who sits all day surrounded
by masses of black hair.

The Elven men are lanky,
are small, discreet, and wise.
The Elven men are hunters
of ermine and of vair.
They look from dusky faces
with faceted red eyes
and make unbreaking bowstrings
out of a maiden's hair.

They steal a cotter's daughter
from out the barnyard straw.
They steal the king's own daughter
who plays beneath the throne.
They take, the Elven men,
without regard for law,
they steal away the daughters
and take them for their own.

The daughters of the Elves
have sorrow-haunted eyes.
They sit beside the waters
and raise their slender hands,
beside the silent waters,
beneath the solemn skies,
and slowly snip their tresses,
strand by strand by strand.

The Elven men returning
from hunt at end of day
skin and sew up their catches
of ermine and of vair.
They dress their tall pale daughters
in skins of white and gray
and stroke, with approving glances,
their massy falls of hair.

Songs for Ophelia

The Heart

He took the heart from beneath her breast
(it shimmered in the bright air);
he displayed it as one displays garnets
and sold it at Vanity Fair.

The mayor bought that heart for his daughter
and, strung on a silver chain,
she wore it over her collarbone
like an iridescent stain.

The mayor's daughter went walking out
and passed a pale young maid
who stood with her eyes on the pavement,
woebegone and mad.

The mayor's daughter clutched at her garments
and kissed her pale young face,
and passers-by saw her weeping
as she ran to the marketplace.

Two hearts, two hearts, have been sold today
from a stall at Vanity Fair,
and they shine on a pin that the princess
has slipped through the loops of her hair,

and on the high road two maidens are wandering,
mad and glad and free,
jeering at passing strangers.
Soon there will be three.

Ravens

Some men are actually ravens.

Oh, they look like men.
Some of them in suits,
some of them in shirts embroidered
with the names of baseball teams,
some in uniforms, fighting in wars we only see
on television.
But underneath, they are ravens.
Look carefully, and you will find their skins of feathers.

Once, I fell in love with a raven man.
I knew that to keep him I had to take his skin,
his skin of feathers, long and black as night,
like ebony, tarmac, licorice, black holes.
I found it (he had taken it off to play baseball)
and hid it in the attic.

He was mine for seven years.

I had to make promises:
not to hurt ravens, to give our children names
like Sky, and Rain Cloud, and Nest-of-Twigs,
spend one night a week in the bole of an old oak tree
that had been hollowed out by who-knows-what.
I had to eat worms. (Yes, I ate worms.)
You do crazy things for raven men.

In return,
he spent six nights a week in my arms.
His black feathers fell around me.
He gave me three children
(Sky, Rain Cloud, Nest-of-Twigs,
whom we called Twiggy).
And I was happy,
which is more than most people achieve.

You know where this is going.
One day, I threw a stone at a raven.
I was not angry, he was not doing anything in particular.
It is just
that raven men are always lost.
Think of it as destiny,
think of it as inevitable.

I was not tired of our nights together,
with the moon gleaming on his feathers.
No.

Or maybe he found his skin in the attic?

Maybe I had taken his skin and he found it,
and he picked three feathers from it
and touched each of our children,
and they flew away together?
Maybe that's how I lost them?

Songs for Ophelia

I don't even remember.

Loving raven men will make you crazy.
In the mornings I see them hurrying to their offices,
the men in suits. And I see them in bars
shouting for their baseball teams, and I see them
on television in wars that have no names,
and I say, that one is a raven man,
and that one, and that one.

Sometimes I stop one and say,
will you send my raven man back to me?
And my raven children?
Some night, when the moon is gleaming,
the way it used to gleam
on long black feathers falling
around my face?

Raven Poem

On the fence sat three ravens.

The first was the raven of night,
whose wings spread over the evening.
On his wings were stars, and in his beak
he carried the crescent moon.

The second was the raven of death,
who eats human hearts. He regarded me
sideways, as birds do. Shoo, I said.
Fly away, old scavenger. I'm not ready
to go with you. Not yet.

The third was my beloved,
who had taken the form of a raven.
Come to me, I said,
when darkness falls, although
I'm afraid you too
will eat my heart.

Death

The night has gathered around me. I think of Death,
who breathes so softly beside my ear, like a lover.
Softly he whispers, "This will soon be over.
You will lay those bones and heavy body down."

I am in love with him because he holds me
so close, much closer than I have ever been held,
and I think that I will never again be cold,
although a wind is blowing in the darkness.

I worry that he does not seem to care
for the sorts of things I packed before I came here:
my friendships and memories. "What do they matter," he asks,
"When you are resting safely in my arms?"

I put my bags on the bank beside the river
and answer him, as the night gathers around,
"Death, you are right. These things do not matter,
not here in your arms. Not here."

The Last Night that She Lived

The last night that she lived,
I scarcely felt her breath.
She wandered, vacant-eyed,
the misty hills of death.
She wandered, while I stayed,
through fogs that canceled sight,
the country of death hid
in a sort of twilight.

I stroked her ragged hair.
She wandered through the whirls
of gray and opaque air,
or opalescent swirls
when the sun shone fair,
but never saw one bough
of forest, nor one mere
of bladed grass, below.

How noiselessly she went!
I wake at night in fear.
Blind country of the bent,
shall one find comfort there?
When soul from form is rent,
do streams run over stones
in valleys of content?
Or dust, on bones?

Dirge for a Lady

Lay her in lavender, all that is left of her;
lavender preserves the lovely and the white.
Sweet clove and cinnamon, like a fine pomander,
lay her in these, the delicate, the slight.

Look how her hands are turned to alabaster,
translucent and tender, and breakable as pain.
Fine every filament, as though a thin spider
had woven her. She's shattered, and shall not arise again.

Rain, do not mourn her, nor rose adorn her.
How frail, this arrangement of elegant dry dust;
one breath would scatter her, one teardrop tatter her.
Think of her softly, and only if you must.

Lay her in lavender, all that is left of her.
Let nothing ravel the final webs of form,
where nor the rain nor roses come, a scented sepulcher,
airless and close, and infinitely calm.

Bal Macabre

Death, playing a mandolin,
asked when I would begin
to join, with Hope and Love, the mad pavane.

They turned in velvet tails,
while antiquated veils
fluttered like wisps of peacock-colored lawn.

I did a pirouette.
Death, in ample jet,
kissed me her hand and smiled indulgently.

I crossed the checkered floor
clutching a battledore
as Art and War were taking toast and tea.

The pillars of that hall,
of quarried marble all,
did nothing but eternally ascend,

a luminescent mist
the hue of amethyst
concealing any place where they might end.

I flung a window wide,
hoping to gaze outside,
and watched a painted landscape crack and flake,

then turned back to the room
where Beauty, with a broom,
was sweeping up the final crumbs of cake.

I leaned upon the wall,
observing the crazed ball,
and saw the grinning figures bow and spin,

then felt myself advance
to join the gruesome dance,
while Death looked on and played a mandolin.

A Haunting

Let her name be written on the shifting air.
Let it roam about the rooms of atmosphere
like a restless ghost in a haunted space.
Let it wander, whispering, ever place to place.

We shall hear it early, when the willows speak
at the crux of springtime, sibilant and weak.
We shall hear it later, fading, far away,
as the oak trees' shadows rustle on the clay.

We shall hear it latest in the sparrow's wing
as she ruffs her feathers, without joy or song,
where the falling winter covers all the brake.
Listen to it moving, spend the night awake.

Listen as it softly ruffles on the ground;
start beneath your covers at the slightest sound.
Once her name was written on the shifting air.
Shiver in the darkness: listen, she is here.

The Ghost

At night, when the others are all
asleep in their beds,
dreaming the incoherent
dreams of the night,
I sit in this room, alone
by the light of the lamp,
and I write.

Are my dreams as incoherent
as theirs, though I sit
awake? Sometimes I think so,
and feel so alone.
There is nothing like the night
to do that – the night
and the moon.

And then sometimes it winks
through the window, I think,
and suddenly I feel
comforted and at ease,
as though the chairs were my friends,
and the windows, and even
the trees.

And I think – philosophical, since
it is night, and the others
are all where they ought to be,
asleep in their beds –

that being a writer is rather
like being a ghost,
which needs

only the night and the lonely
light of the lamp,
and the friendly chairs – in short,
to haunt a room
where incomprehensible dreams
can cohere and
take form.

Songs for Ophelia

Binnorie

What is it about being made into a harp,
your bones as smooth as poplar, about being strung
with your own hair, golden or black or brown,
that presents such an appropriate allegory
for being a woman, and therefore an instrument
of fathers, husbands, or sons? Or is it rather
an allegory for being a poet, which is
a different thing altogether, I like to think,
although poetry can command you like a father,
berate you like a husband, and abandon
you like any number of sons?

Theodora Goss

Narcissus

Let the waters pass
and let him gaze on them, dreaming,
as a girl would gaze in her glass.
The relentlessly streaming

years will expose
the ghastly and elegant bone,
over which even the rose
will wither soon.

The birds will come,
sparrows among them, and the jay,
and as though each piece were a crumb
carry it away.

The Naiad

She came on the verge of winter
to the old King's castle gate.
She seemed a ragged beggar
half overcome by fate:
the drifting snow hid in her hair
and her limbs wore tattered weeds,
and the wildness of angry waters was in her stare,
and reeds.

But for that she was ragged,
bound on her head we saw,
set in a fillet of gold,
a green gem without flaw
that would purchase the title of many a queen,
and the young Prince perceived
that her eyes were the colour of the sea's mid-morning gleam
through reeds.

The old King ordered ermine
to cover her white breast,
and twenty high-born maidens
conducted her to rest
under coverlets stuffed with the swan's white down,
and I not the only there
who would trade broad acres of land to drift and drown
in her hair.

Her rags became bright raiment
embroidered with gold and pearls.
Floated her filmy garments,
scattered her black curls,
when within the moonlit courtyard danced
the royal maids and men,
and the young Prince took her in his arms and turned
and spun.

She was small and daintily fashioned,
with cheeks like polished stone.
On a harp her fingers flashed,
as quietly she would croon
a wordless song like the sea beneath
a gray and windy sky,
lonely as cries of gulls, and her final breath
was a sigh.

I brought her a snow-white rose.
She placed it in her hair
and smiled, but in her eyes
lingered unshed tears.
The young Prince brought her a snow-white steed,
pliable as a wand,
straight as a cliff. She cried and hid her head
in her hands.

The moon wore the face of a mother
over the slumbering waves.
The chill of the ending year
drew the old King close to the flames.
But she stared out the window where the sea
slept under wraith-like clouds
and hid her sorrowing face in her hair and freely
sobbed.

She crept from the hall where the monarch
murmured in his dreams.
Silently through the arches
in the light of the full moon's beams,
she tiptoed through the castle gate
and with a silver key,
let herself out unto the shingle, jubilantly
free.

No one saw she had gone
but the young Prince and I.
He thought he tracked her alone,
I followed them both like a spy.
I saw her stand at the edge of the strand
and her ankles were wet with spray.
Her small bare foot left an imprint in the sand,
then away

she moved upon the billows
and the young Prince, with a cry,
followed her into the waves,
floundering through that sea
as a young bird flaps through turbulent air,
and choked upon the spume
until . . . she turned and caught and with tender care,
through the foam,

brought him over the water,
laid him on the sand,
touched his tangled hair
with her glistening hand,
leaning, softly kissed his mouth
with love's tenderness,
felt the straggling breath within his breast,
one caress

to ascertain life was there
and for a last farewell.
I saw her floating hair
spread upon the swell
like a scrap of seaweed tossed and borne
by the tidal flow.
Long I saw her white hands tread the foam,
then go.

Songs for Ophelia

When day was in the sky,
the young Prince awoke,
on his own pillow lay
among his own folk,
and sighed but never spoke again
of the sea-maiden comely
as wind and rain who grew heartsick for her crashing
sea.

Song of the Daughters

When the world was young and her daughters were slender and fair,
and danced on the shores of the world in the sea-salt air,
with strands of seaweed ribbanding their hair,

the only sound was the surf and the clacking of shells
they rattled in woven bags, the sound of the swells
and the sound of their voices like clashing silver bells.

They sang of sand and salt, and a clear soft strain
of the roses that grow on dunes, and their harsh refrain
was the lashing of waves in the froth of a falling rain.

Their shoulders were bare and translucent, like new-laid pearls,
their garments of film, like the fabric each wave unfurls,
and they danced on the strand when the world was young, her girls.

I saw them once, one night when the moon lay cold
over the shifting waves, where the waters rolled,
hobbling together, grown silent, bent, and old.

The Singer

The songs are done, said the singer,
and he broke the strings of the lute.
The host gazed about with anger,
the guests grew mazed and mute.
But the singer stepped from his chains,
and as he passed them by,
a rankness rotted the grains
and the yellow wine grew wry.
The host, he cursed the fates,
and the guests left all too soon,
while the singer stepped through the gates
into the wide, sweet noon.
He sang a song to the hills
without aid of instrument;
he heard their echoed trills,
and then he turned and went.

And since the singer left,
we jangle and we start:
all toneless now and reft,
the lutestrings of the heart.

CPSIA information can be obtained at www.ICGtesting.com
Printed in the USA
BVOW07s1734130714

359032BV00001B/3/P